BE

By . Lisa . Everest .

MAPLE
PUBLISHERS

Be

Author: Lisa Everest

Copyright © Lisa Everest (2025)

The right of Lisa Everest to be identified as author of this work has been asserted by the author in accordance with section 77 and 78 of the Copyright, Designs and Patents Act 1988.

First Published in 2025

ISBN: 978-1-83538-548-7 (Paperback)

Book layout by:
    Maple Publishers
    www.maplepublishers.com

Published by:
    Maple Publishers
    Fairbourne Drive,
    Atterbury,
    Milton Keynes,
    MK10 9RG, UK
    www.maplepublishers.com

A CIP catalogue record for this title is available from the British Library.

All rights reserved. No part of this book may be reproduced or translated by any form or by any means, electronic or mechanical, including photocopying, recording or by any information storage and retrieval system without written permission from the author.

The book is a work of fiction. Unless otherwise indicated, all the names, characters, places and incidents are either the product of the author's imagination or used in a fictitious manner. Any resemblance to actual people living or dead, events or locales is entirely coincidental, and the Publisher hereby disclaims any responsibility for them.

THIS LITTLE BOOK HAS BEEN DESIGNED SO THAT YOU CAN POP IT IN YOU'R BAG OR POCKET.
IT CAN TRAVEL WITH YOU, IT CAN STAY NEXT TO YOUR BED.
YOU CAN EVEN COLOUR IT IN.
A LOVING REMINDER TO STAY CONNECTED. STAY IN TUNE TO THE EARTH AND THE ENERGY THATS CREATED IN AND AROUND US!
I HOPE THESE PAGES BRING YOU THE CHANCE TO PAUSE, A MOMENT TO REFLECT AND CONNECT.

. REFLECT .

. CONNECT .

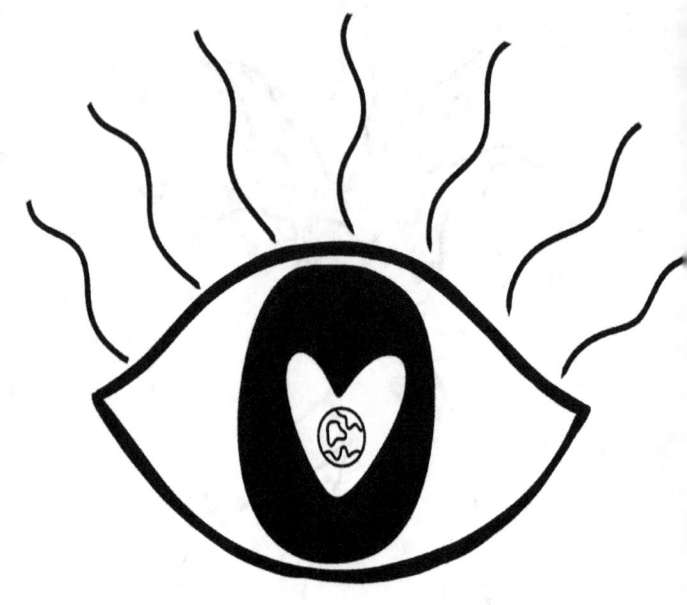

LOVE IS POWER. LOVE IS THE ULTIMATE POWER. LOVE IS EVERYTHING. OUR HEART CENTER.

SENSES CREATE
CONSCIOUSNESS

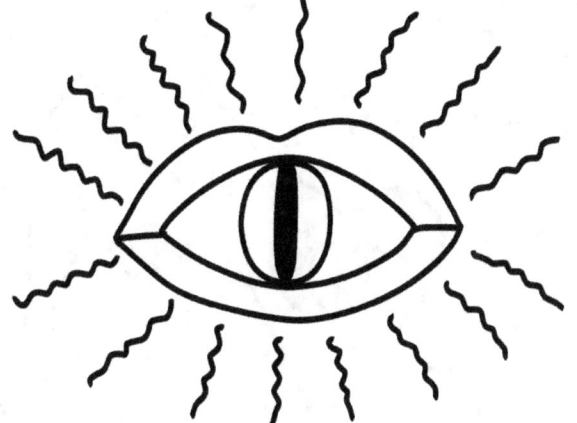

CONNECTIONS.   UNITY.

FOREVER CHANGING MOON

AS HER FACE CHANGES SO DO OUR EMOTIONS.
A REMINDER THAT NOTHING STAYS THE SAME. NOT EVEN US!

To have great love in our hearts
is one of the greatest feelings of
all.
This power takes over all things.
Its ability to propel us up to a
higher being.
Flourishing all energy with in.
A sensation, a zest, a wanting for
all things and for our own being
to feel connected.
A belonging, a confidence, an
excitment for life and its truest
beauty.
A fullness in your chest so intense
you can feel your heart expanding.
Love is tenderness, patience,
compassion.
Love is kind, caring, energetic,
soothing, fuzzy and warm.
Love is friendly.
Love is your friend ♡

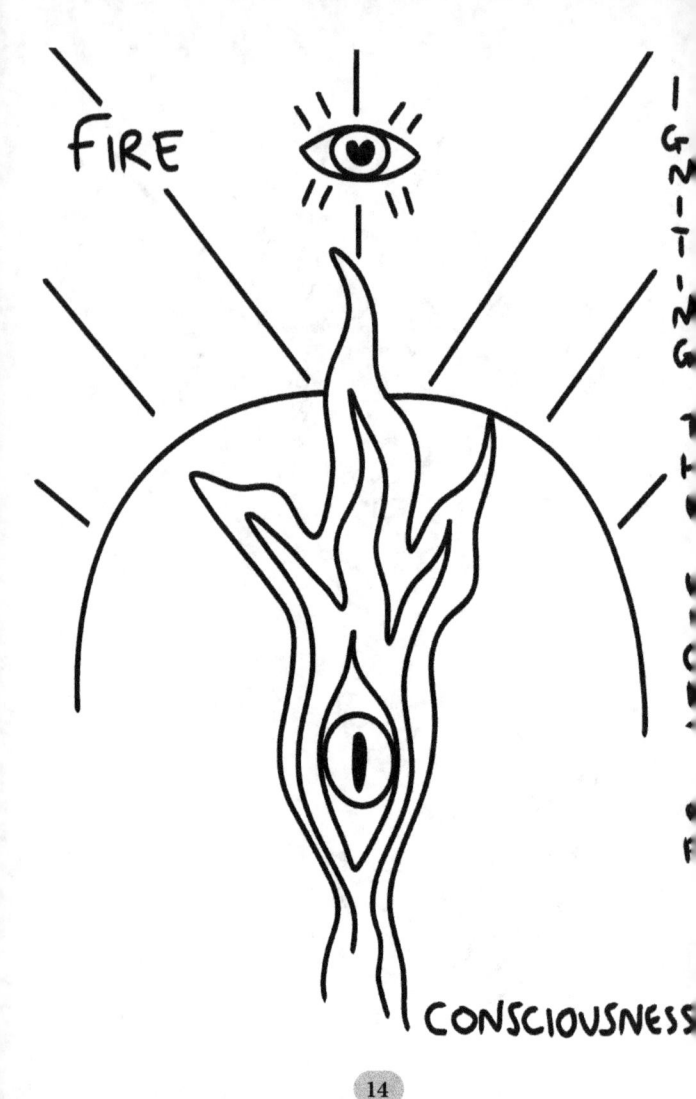

MAY THE MOVEMENT OF THE TIDES, THE RUNNING RIVERS, THE CHANGING CYCLES PROVIDE CHANGE AND GROWTH IN OUR LIVES.

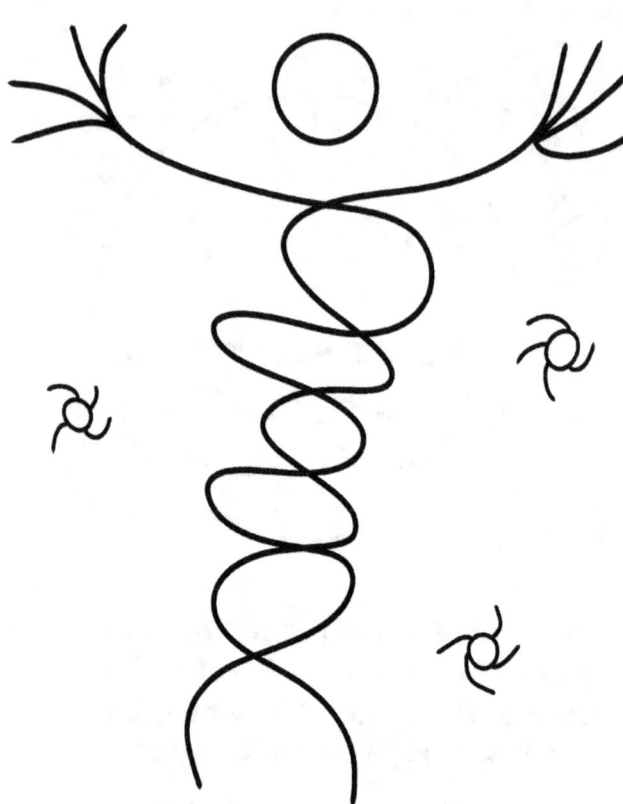

TO BE GROUNDED IS THE HERE AND NOW !!!

TO GROUND IS TO ARRIVE.

TO GROUND IS TO EMBRACE.

TO GROUND IS TO BE INTOUCH.

GROUNDING IS POWER ON ITS OWN.

GROUNDING IS A FEELING OF BEING SAFE.

GROUNDING CREATES STILLNESS.

ONE SPACE, ONE TIME.

THAT, THAT HAS ROOTS WILL ENDURE.

THE ROOT CHAKRA IS <u>EVERYTHING</u>.

IT LEADS US TO ALL CONNECTION.
WE ARE ONE WHEN GROUNDED

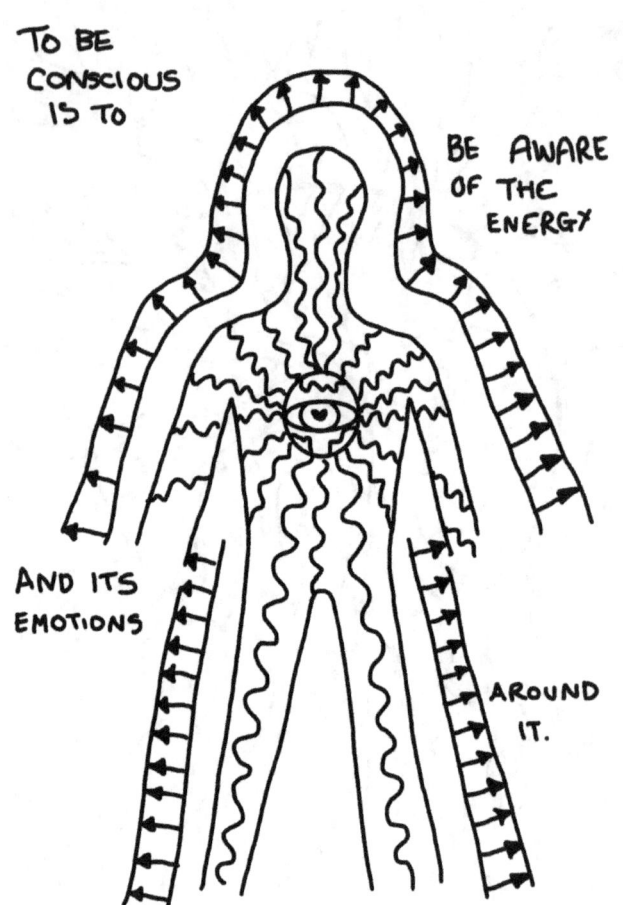

ENERGY THROUGH OUR BODY

BREATH
BLUE
THROAT CHAKRA

EARTH
HEART CHAKRA
GREEN

YELLOW
SOLAR PLEXUS
ORANGE
SACRAL CHAKRA
FIRE
RED
ROOT CHAKRA

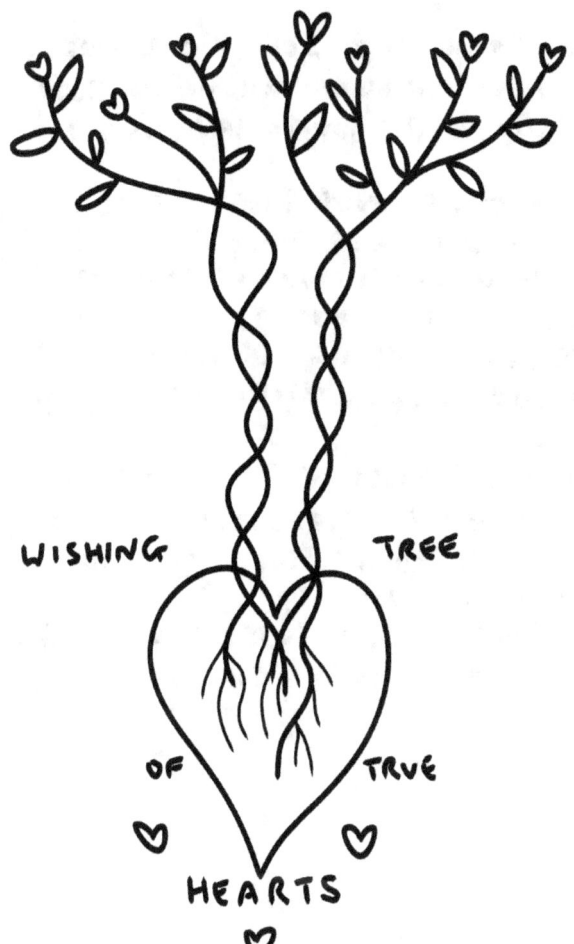

TO GROUND IS TO ACCEPT OUR BODY.
TO FEEL OUR BODY, VALIDATE OUR BODY,
TO LOVE OUR BODY, TO HAVE AND TO
BE.
WITH OUT CHANGE THERE IS NO GROWTH.
LET GO AND CREATE FLOW.
WE MOVE FROM MOMENT TO MOMENT,
THOUGHT TO THOUGHT.
WE ARE LIVING IN MOTION.
PLEASURE IS IMORTANT FOR SPIRIT AND
SOUL.
PLEASURE REJUVENATES OUR SPIRIT.
SIMPLE SIMPLE PLEASURES.
EMOTIONS PROMOTE THE EVOLUTION OF
OUR CONSCIOUSNESS.
EMOTIONS HELP US TO MOVE OUT OF THE
BODY AND IN TO THE CONSCIOUS MIND.

THAT MOVES THE EARTH BELOW AND FIRE ABOVE

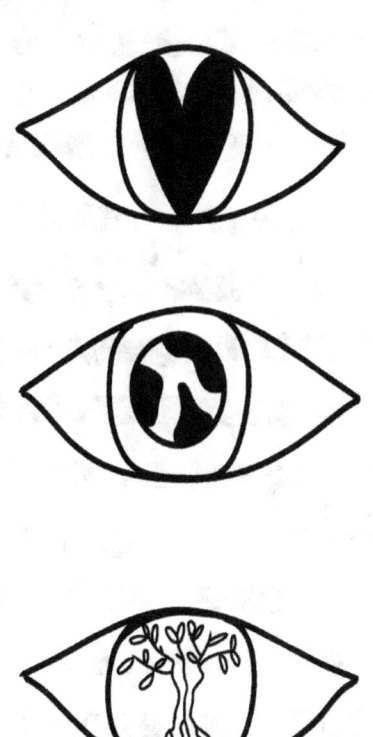

SOUND SACRED SPIN CHAKRAS MAKING UP RISING BUILDING MOVING

TO BE GROUNDED IS TO BE STILL

· REFLECT ·

· CONNECT ·

BOOK HAND
MADE BY
LISA EVEREST
lijaeverest@gmail.com